GIRL POWER

The Smart Woman's Handbook

KITTY M.

SUMMERSDALE

Copyright © Kitty Malone 1997

All rights reserved.

No part of this book may be reproduced by any means, nor transmitted,
nor translated into a machine language
without the written permission of the publisher.

Summersdale Publishers
46 West Street
Chichester
West Sussex
PO19 1RP   England

ISBN 1 84024 021 0

A CIP catalogue record for this book is available from the British Library.

Printed and bound in Great Britain.

TO MY FELLOW SUCCESSFUL, SMART AND SEXY WOMEN

Especially...

My mother (thank you), my godmother Sally (the best a girl could have), Xenia (doctor), the Honourable Eleanor Flower (solicitor), Zoe (PR fashion diva), Rebecca (business magazine editor), Chloe (recruitment consultant), Sarah H (journalist), Joanne Rose (boy band groupie), Catherine (sportswoman and tea at the Ritz girl), Sarra (multimedia PR guru and party organiser), Fiona (graphic designer) and last, but by no means least, Emma and Annie (rising publishing stars and sources of inspiration).

GIRL POWER

The Smart Woman's Handbook

Welcome to the smart woman's handbook! Smart women are simply never at a loss for words and this indispensable little book will prove just that.

Here, the most famous women in the world get down to the bare essentials and talk about all the important things in every girl's life...money, men, parties, fashion, sex and much more.

You have already been smart enough to buy my book, or perhaps someone equally smart gave it to you.

Learn your lessons from these wise and wicked women as they offer you their words of wisdom.

It's time to pay attention...

THE ART OF
GIRL POWER

Before I allow the leading ladies to take centre stage, I am going to say a little about what I think *Girl Power* means for today's smart woman.

Girl Power is not all about a generation of girls who kickbox their way around town, destroying all the pathetic menfolk that get in their way.

Aggression and arrogance are not attractive qualities in my opinion.

If we smart women get too carried away with our *Girl Power*, then we might just end up with a generation of terrified, wimpy men on our hands.

Or maybe even in them.

I am the first to admit that I like men rather a lot. I really do, and so I do not want them to live in fear of asking me out and buying me a drink.

Girl Power is not about intimidation.

True *Girl Power* is letting the man think that things are going just as he wants them to, while you, naturally, have everything already beautifully planned out from beginning to end.

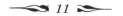

Men may well be still playing the game, but remember, it is always the smart women who know the score.

Girl Power is all about using those precious feminine qualities that we have been blessed with.

There is no point trying to be a man's equal when we are already his superior!

Smart women always have the upper hand, they know what they want and they are brilliant at getting it.

The art of *Girl Power* is not all about desperately flaunting your sexuality and asserting your rights.

It is about understanding that your most feminine attributes can be your most beguiling.

All the women in this book are fabulously feminine.

They are very successful, very smart and very sexy.

They have confidence, intelligence, humour, allure, passion.

They have true *Girl Power*.

So, lie back, think of yourself and enjoy this celebration of *Girl Power* as we explore everything from teabags to tiaras...

Get glamorous, get gorgeous, get glorious and get with the girls!

LIFE

Smart women are completely in control of their lives. Sophie Tucker, an American singer, provides some great guidelines,

'From birth to age 18 a girl needs good parents. From 18 to 35 she needs good looks. From 35 to 55 she needs a good personality and from 55 on she needs good cash.'

Wonderful. Follow these rules and you have every smart woman's credentials.

However, rules, as we well know, are there for breaking,

'If you obey all the rules you miss all the fun,' said Katharine Hepburn.

I just can't help agreeing with her.

Smart women break the rules, but always blame somebody else.

Smart women like getting into trouble and out of it.

Smart girls are bad girls.

Their diaries will be full from daylight to midnight.

Anne Frank they most definitely are not,

'It's the good girls who keep the diaries; the bad girls never have the time,' said Tallulah Bankhead, the American actress.

Fill your filofax with fun but be careful.

Your diary is strictly for appointments only.

Mae West warns all smart women,

'Keep a diary and one day it will keep you.'

Your life should ideally consist of one very good and lucrative job, one very good and lucrative man (not essential, but useful) and several very good girlfriends who will be just as loyal and loving as you are.

PARTIES

When it comes down to it, life for a smart woman is really one big party.

As a smart woman you will naturally be seen in all the right places.

Film premiers, festivals and royal weddings.

Celebrity bashes, book launches and Grand Prix meetings.

Polo events, society balls and pop video previews.

Grand Slam events, Commissioning Balls, club openings.

New restaurants' first nights in cosmopolitan capitals and all the fashion collections.

These are just a few of the ones I attended last week.

Your guru is Nan Kempner, probably the most invited and most partied smart woman in the Western world who famously said,

'Darling, I wouldn't miss the opening of an envelope.'

It may just be that, in some hideous oversight, your name has been left off the invitation list.

Find out who the host is, ring them up and tell them how much you are looking forward to seeing them.

Then they will be expecting you.

Here's another tried and tested method for getting you over the threshold.

If the party is not being held in the height of summer, then arrive without a coat, in a fragile, flimsy little number.

Buy some cigarettes and clutch them visibly in your hand.

Arrive late and walk confidently past the doorman, flutter your eyelashes and march in.

If stopped, tell him you have been out to buy
more of your favourite brand.

He will hardly imagine that such a smart woman
would turn up without a beautiful coat draped
over her chilly shoulders.

Or put on a sexy French accent, shrug your shoulders and tell him you are so very sorry and you won't do it again.

Once inside, procure yourself a bottle of champagne and people will welcome you with open arms.

And remember, the definition of a flirt is a woman who thinks that it is every man for herself and there's nothing wrong with that.

Smart women know how to dress up and dine out (preferably at someone else's expense).

Smart women should be able to party all night long and still make lunch with their girlfriends the next day.

Smart women will certainly drink but should heed Dorothy Parker's advice,

'One more drink and I'll be under the host.'

Although this may be an attractive proposition at the time, things are often all too different in the cold, clear light of morning.

Drunk women are NOT attractive. One more vodka may help you relax but one too many and you will live to regret it.

Parties may well be of your own creation. There are so many party possibilities.

Have parties for your best girlfriends, potential pulls or useful contacts.

They can be wonderful if organised properly.

Fill your fridge as if every day holds the possibility of a party that evening.

Crates of champagne, bottles of chilled Chardonnay, cans of lager (for the boys), orange juice and Lucozade (for the morning after), a selection of dips, bags of cherries, bars of chocolate.

Marks & Spencer's sticky toffee puddings and chocolate mousse for indulgence.

The fridge is also a handy place to keep beauty products especially in the hot summer months.

Keep eye masks in there, lipsticks and body cream as it feels divine when it's cold. If it's vanilla scented then all the better...

For the rest of the kitchen, always have several phone numbers of well reputed takeaway establishments to hand (just in case).

Joan Plowright suggests getting someone else to cook so you can be the perfect hostess and pay attention to all your guests,

'I love entertaining. I have someone else to do the cooking; that's why.'

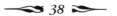

And if the hired help is a tall, dark, handsome man who does wondrous things with various implements, then so much the better!

MONEY

To fund your party habit you will need cash.

Ah, how I love the feeling of crisp, hot-off-the-press banknotes.

Smart women should always have a little money of their own as financial independence is, I think, necessary for us girls.

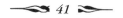

However, the trust fund or piggy-bank (according to your background) should really be left untouched.

There should always be a man around who is only too keen to be your private banker.

As Aristotle Onassis so wisely pointed out,

'If women didn't exist then all the money in the world would have no meaning.'

Of course, no smart woman should marry solely for money.

However, Jane Austen certainly had a point when she said,

'It is a truth universally acknowledged that a single man in possession of a good fortune must be in want of a wife.'

A man with a pair of sodden jodhpurs (think of Colin Firth in *Pride and Prejudice*) **and** a good fortune.

Now, **that** is true husband material. And make sure that it is of ample proportions.

His fortune that is.

Lana Turner, the American film actress, said that,

'A successful man is one who makes more money than his wife can spend. A successful woman is one who can find such a man.'

Perfect the art of letting the man provide the money for your wonderful time, whether you're with him or not.

And the men **will** enjoy spending those crisp banknotes on you (you're worth it, after all).

It makes them feel generous and they live in hope that they may just get a little something in return.

So, if he asks what sort of books you are interested in then say cheque books.

But remember - men and money can slip and slide through your fingers only too easily if you're not careful.

And, if you choose to bid him a fond farewell, then don't worry if you feel a streak of materialism creeping in.

Get something to remember him by.

Always say goodbye just after your birthday and definitely after Christmas. That way you make sure you get a good present.

The marvellous Marilyn Monroe had a sound piece of advice for all smart women,

'I always say a kiss on the hand might feel very good, but a diamond tiara lasts forever.'

You'll look stunning in it and you can wear it to all those parties.

HUSBANDS

For the smart woman of today a loving, devoted man, or even just a husband, is something you may choose to acquire.

Husbands can be adoring and attentive. However, they can also be a little like children - demanding and disobedient.

Zsa Zsa Gabor warns us,

'Husbands are like fires - they go out when unattended.'

So, make sure that your man wouldn't dare. You need a man that matches up.

And a match made in heaven should be a meeting of minds and money.

Behind every glamorous and gifted couple there is one very smart woman - Cherie Blair and Tony Blair, Ruth Rogers (proprietor of the very hip River Cafe) and the architect Lord Richard Rogers, Patsy Kensit and Liam Gallagher.

And although a man with a passion for old bones
may not set your heart pounding, Agatha Christie
points out,

*'An archaeologist is the best husband any woman
can have. The older she gets, the more he is
interested in her.'*

Choosing a husband is as difficult as choosing a dress. You have to try out loads before you find one that really fits you.

Husbands should be chosen with great care and attention.

Remember that you are exchanging the attentions of many men for the inattention of just one.

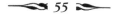

Of course, your standards will naturally be extremely high.

When you do find a man who would make a good husband, you may well find that he already is.

I would advise against marital affairs as sharing your chosen one is not the smartest of ideas.

However, you could follow Britt Ekland's advice, which may help ease any guilt,

'I say I don't sleep with married men, but what I mean is that I don't sleep with happily married men.'

Beware. Love your neighbour, but don't get caught.

A man cannot give you all the attention you deserve if he is still doing his best to displease someone else.

Your fortunate spouse will be courageous, noble, powerful, supportive, trustworthy, respectful, flattering and virile.

At the very least he should be utterly dutiful, truly devoted and a bit of a devil if he is to last a lifetime - his, that is.

MEN

Magnetic, magnificent and marriageable.

Muscular, masterful and memorable.

These are the men who will be captivated by smart women.

Unfortunately, your charms may also attract less appealing specimens.

These should be treated with sympathy, but ultimately deterred.

Smart women do not always need a man if they are to succeed in life.

Men can frequently be more hindrance then help.

So they sometimes need a helping hand.

Remember that men are there for your pleasure.

With a few nudges in the right direction, they should perform well, as Jilly Cooper says,

'The male is a domestic animal which, if treated with firmness and kindness, can be trained to do most things.'

Indeed, Elizabeth Taylor has noted that,

'Some of my best leading men have been dogs and horses.'

Unfortunately, if he does not give 100% at the beginning then it is unlikely that he ever will.

Marlene Dietrich says perceptively,

'Most women set out to try to change a man, and when they have changed him they do not like him.'

As a smart woman you will attract many males and they will all be doing their best to impress you.

Some words of advice from a confirmed serial monogamist, Zsa Zsa Gabor,

'Macho does not prove mucho.'

Men cannot think straight as they always have curves on their mind.

They find it difficult to keep their hands to themselves. This is understandable as you will be looking gorgeous.

Suggest that he keeps his hands on his cheque book instead.

Otherwise, as sensible Mae West says,

'Give a man a free hand and he will run it all over you.'

While you wait for the right man to come along you may as well have fun with some wrong ones.

Do not attempt to convince him that his intentions are serious until you have concluded that you wish them to be.

A good man will be hard to hold on to.

Make the most of the man - do with him what you will but, please, make occasional allowances for their fragile egos.

Smart women, such as Anna Ford, queen of the anchorwomen, understand that,

'It is the men who face the biggest problems in the future, adjusting to their new and complicated role.'

This is why it is important not to terrify them into submission.

They need reassurance that a smart woman does appreciate a smart man.

The men of today are quite overawed by our feminine ways but remain sure that one day they will finally understand us.

Smart women naturally know better.

The right man for you will be a very special man indeed.

Let him into your car, office, swimming pool, bathroom and bedroom but not without careful consideration...

SEX

There is no doubt about it - sex feels good - especially when the man has a dirty mind, hungry lips and a desire to satisfy you.

As a smart woman you will have chosen a prime specimen to join you in your pleasuredome of passion.

Check he doesn't slobber first,

'Anyone who's a great kisser I'm always interested in,' said Cher.

Assess his status. If you are at his castle then the risk of being caught by the butler may perk things up a little.

But don't mistake the wallet in his pocket for anything else.

Tina Brown, socialite and old editor of Tatler, gets excited by a title,

'I could fall for a duke - they are a great aphrodisiac.'

The most important thing of all is that whatever you do and whoever you do it with, as a smart woman you will feel good at the time and you will feel good afterwards.

Sex in a great relationship is smart. Sex *and* a great relationship is also an option as long as you don't get caught. It is your choice.

Get the man doing the work as those sexy Spice
Girls tell us,

'Use it, prove it, show me how good you are.'

Never, ever do things you don't want to. But don't
be scared to experiment.

Some women feel a lot more in control with a pair of handcuffs and a silk scarf to hand - at least you know where he will be for the next couple of hours.

Go for self-gratification if he isn't up to your demands. Lie down and think of yourself.

There is nothing more wonderful than a sexy, smart woman, as Sophia Loren knew,

'Sex appeal is 50% what you have got and 50% what people think you have got.'

As a smart woman it is up to you how much of yourself you want to reveal.

Smart women decide what they want, how they want it and who they want it with.

Sex expert Shere Hite says,

'All too many men still believe that what feels good to them is automatically what feels good to a woman.'

So, be gentle with him and if he asks if you're faking it then just tell him you're practising for next time.

And if your Adonis is only around for an evening then, please, do not spoil it by morning-after-one-night-stand guilt.

If you feel you must do something afterwards, you could always ask him his name.

Choose a post-coital cigar rather than pillow talk -
it looks damn sexy and is probably far more
satisfactory.

And remember,

*'Sex is important, but by no means the only
important thing in life,'* as Mary Whitehouse said.

Besides, sex can get awfully messy. If you're
frolicking then take off your attire first.

*'Sex is a bad thing because it rumples the
clothes,'* said Jackie Onassis.

And we girls know that a smart woman always has style, whether she is in her clothes or out of them...

STYLE

Style is a little like sex. Some people have it and some people don't.

If you don't have it then you can buy it.

Today a girl is spoilt for choice - high street, designer boutiques, secondhand stores and hire shops all burst at the seams with glamour.

But do not ever become a slave to fashion gurus - indeed, do not become a slave to anyone.

Margaret Thatcher may have worn the trousers but she acknowledged,

'I haven't the figure for jeans.'

If you've got it, flaunt it, as the saying goes, but plunging necklines and crotch-skimming skirts should never, ever be worn together - unless you frequent street corners.

Sophia Loren, Italian icon, remarked,

'Today a man can see practically the whole woman at a single glance. It's swallowing a meal at one mouthful.'

Swallowing in one can sometimes be just too much.

Be a tease and offer a taster.

Leave something to the imagination and get them begging for more.

Smart women do not need to follow fashion when they can set the style.

Know yourself,

'The legs aren't so beautiful, I just know what to do with them,' said Marlene Dietrich.

Classy clothes will do wonders for your figure and a shopping spree is far more fun than three hours in the gym.

If only men could be more like clothes - flattering, figure-hugging and well hung.

But more important than your Armani suit or your Gucci handbag is your inner poise.

Style comes from within.

Diana Vreeland, American fashion guru, said,

'The only real elegance is in the mind. If you've got that, the rest really follows from it.'

It's all about attitude. If you feel good then you'll look good.

The world and most of the men in it will be at your feet.

All you need now is a little *Girl Power...*

POWER

Take a little trip through history and you soon realise that women have really put themselves on top.

After all, it's a good position to be in. Boudicea, Elizabeth I, Margaret Thatcher, Madonna to name but a few.

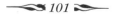

Women got the vote and have their say thanks to
Emily Pankhurst,

*'If civilisation is to advance at all in the future it
must be through the help of women...women with
the full power to work their will in society.'*

A woman at full strength is like a cup of tea - refreshing, revitalising, hot and sweet.

Being compared with Typhoo may not seem that complimentary, but Nancy Reagan said,

'A woman is like a teabag - only in hot water do you realise how strong she is.'

And if Glenda Jackson, actress and politician, invites you round for tea, then be prepared,

'If I'm too strong for some people, that's their problem.'

But you don't have to be a power-crazed dominatrix.

Some go for the dog collar and whip approach but each to their own.

A little bit of patience and some intuition goes a long way - both in the bedroom and in the office.

Margaret Thatcher knew this very well,

'I am extraordinarily patient, provided I get my own way in the end.'

And who would argue with her?

Mrs T took the men by the balls and stayed on top for a considerable length of time.

Get on top and stay there. Roseanne Barr says that power is there for the taking,

'The thing that women have got to learn is that nobody gives you power. You just take it.'

Get it and keep it.

Smart women work hard but they remember to play hard too.

Recognise that you have your limits and don't go beyond them, unless of course the offer is simply too good to turn down.

Take on what you can manage, take on a little bit more and then push yourself just that bit further.

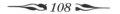

Your power comes from self-belief not a desperately short skirt (although this may help sometimes).

Harriet Rubin, author of *The Princessa*, comments,

'To get what they want - the aim of power - women have to stop trying to ape men and start to act more like women.'

Be yourself.

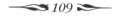

THE ESSENTIAL LIST FOR SMART WOMEN

KITTY'S KIT

TOOTHBRUSH

For after lunch, dinner, too much garlic, fellatio
and for fresh breath at all times. Also useful for
holding up your hair.

NAIL VARNISH

Fabulous for laddered tights but also for gluing in
lenses of glasses, as well as for making nails shiny
and less likely to break.

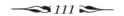

NAIL FILE

Good for broken nails and for getting rid of dead skin on your feet (most unattractive in strappy sandals).

HAIRSPRAY

Also a good form of self-defence when twinned with a lighter in James Bond style.

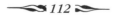

LIP BALM

To keep them soft, sweet and kissable. Also good
for rubbing on dry skin.

LIPLINER

For retouching your lips before someone else
does. Doubles up as a pen.

A POWDER COMPACT

Use the mirror to see the people behind you and
the powder to prevent a shiny nose.

FREE SHAMPOO AND
PERFUME SAMPLES

In case you unexpectedly are unable to return
home to your bathroom cabinet...

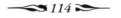

ADDRESS AND
PHONE BOOK

Essential for inserting new ones and
remembering the old ones.

LONDON A - Z

So you never get lost and always turn up
ten minutes late.

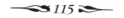

A FULLY CHARGED
MOBILE PHONE

For ringing friends, taxis, takeaways and for
receiving important calls from work and men.

YOUR E-MAIL ADDRESS AND
BUSINESS CARDS

Vital when networking at business events
and parties.

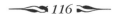

AN UP-TO-DATE CV AND CHEWING GUM

In case you get stuck in a lift with a company
director or devastatingly gorgeous man.

HAIRBRUSH, CONDOMS, TAMPONS, SAFETY PINS and A CHANGE OF UNDERWEAR

Should you get lucky in the lift - but necessary
wherever you are.

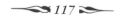

SWISS ARMY KNIFE

Mainly for the bottle opener. Also, the knife for
self-defence and opening letters, the optical
screwdriver for mending glasses and the scissors
for stray hairs and for trimming nails.

CIGARETTES AND LIGHTER

For offering to handsome men, for supplying
impoverished girlfriends and
for generally being cool.

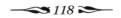

A PEN

Preferably not a Bic biro, as it doesn't look very
stylish when pulled out of your bag. For writing
down all those contacts and for anything else that
catches your eye.

A PENPOINT TORCH

So you can find you contact lenses and
things left under the bed.

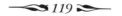

CHOCOLATE

For energy, for enjoying with a cup of coffee, to share, and to prove that you're not on a diet.

A MINIATURE OF YOUR FAVOURITE SPIRIT

For train travel (just buy the mixer in the buffet) and for a quick adrenalin boost.

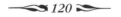

A SCARF

For tying up your hair, for being tied up with, for
making your outfit look different the next day and
useful as a sarong in times of hot weather.

SUNGLASSES

Think Jackie O, think sunshine, think ex-boyfriend
in the same bar, think the morning after...

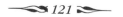

*'You're not too smart -
I like that in a man.'*

Kathleen Turner

AND TO ALL THE MEN
WHO MAKE MY RESEARCH SUCH A PLEASURE

Especially...

My father (thank you), Stewart and Alastair (for being smart enough to employ me), Rob (cake boy and editor-in-chief), Russell (for selling me), James and Charlie Thurstan (honorary brothers and the two most handsome men in the British Army), Divine Dan (the third most handsome), Tom Morton (the most handsome man in the Royal Navy, after my father), Richard Joseph (international publisher and 40 a night man), Jamie (juicy journalist), Dom (the best man to go shopping with), Jason (a hard man to hold onto), David (my favourite dirty, distinguished man), Jules (Notting Hill bad boy) and last, but never, ever least, Alex (for being smashing and always a source of inspiration).

Other Humour Books from Summersdale

How To Chat-up Women
Stewart Ferris   £4.99

How To Chat-up Men
Amy Mandeville   £4.99

How To Stay Married
Dick Hills   £4.99

Chat-up Lines and Put Downs
Stewart Ferris   £3.99

101 Uses for a Losing Lottery Ticket
Shovel/Nadler   £3.99

101 Ways To Spend Your Lottery Millions
Jenny Humphreys   £3.99

Men! Can't Live with them, Can't live with them
Tania Golightly   £3.99

Kama Sutra For One
O'Nan and P. Palm   £3.99

Paws For Thought:
Another Purrfect Day £3.99

Paws For Thought:
It's A Dog's Life   £3.99

Available from all
good bookshops.